MW00790619

A BIBLICAL
SURVEY

by

R. Levy-Lang Cohen

ACADEMIC PUBLISHERS

ISBN: 978-1-9885575-0-2

Published in New Zealand

A catalogue record for this book is available from the National Library of New Zealand.

Kei te pātengi raraunga o Te Puna Mātauranga o Aotearoa te whakarārangi o tēnei pukapuk

Contents

CHAPTER 1

Introduction to the Bible

What Is the Bible?

The Christian Bible is a collection of sixty-six books divided into two "canons" (defined as closed collections of authoritative works). The first thirty-nine books comprise the Hebrew Bible, also known as the Tanakh, Jewish scriptures, or Christian Old Testament. This collection is followed by the twenty-seven books of the New Testament, which completes the Christian Bible.

Although there are different ways of numbering or organizing the biblical books, for this textbook, we will follow the traditional English order, which divides the Jewish scriptures into three parts: seventeen historical books, five poetic books, and seventeen prophetic books. The first five are especially important, as they comprise the Torah or Pentateuch (Greek for "five scrolls"), the books that describe the formation of Israel from the creation of the world to the giving of the Law of Israel to

Moses. These books are often called the "Law of Moses." The other twelve historical books tell the remaining history of Israel and Judah and are followed by five poetic masterpieces of ancient Hebrew literature. As with the historical books, the prophetic corpus is divided into five "Major Prophets," and twelve "Minor Prophets," a distinction made based on the length of the books.

In the traditional Jewish tradition, the Hebrew Bible has a different order to the books. For the beginning student of biblical studies, the difference in the order of the Bible may be confusing. The traditional Hebrew order of these books is significantly different, dividing the Hebrew Bible into three sections. These sections are the Torah, Nevi'im ("Prophets"), and Ketuvim ("Writings"). Four of the historical books (counting Samuel and Kings as one book apiece) are counted as part of the Nevi'im along with four of the prophetic books: Isaiah, Jeremiah, Ezekiel, and "the twelve" (the twelve minor prophets counted as one book). The Ketuvim contains the remaining eleven books. Some Christian traditions also include additional books in their Old Testament. These books are called "deuterocanonical" within those traditions, while Protestant Christians call them the "Apocrypha."

The New Testament is divided into four sections: the four Gospels, the book of Acts, the twenty-one Epistles, and Revelation. This order is the same across all languages.

Putting the Bible on the Map

The geography of the Bible in modern times is a geopolitical hotspot. For generations, the area has been subject to rebellions, empires, and conflict. Geographically, the Bible focuses upon the small strip of land on the eastern side of the Mediterranean Sea, roughly corresponding to today's Israel. The broader context of the Bible includes the region and nations of the Ancient Near East, along with Greece and Rome and their empires.

A study of the Bible for any student includes understanding the overarching narrative of the Tanakh and New Testament. Both of these two cannons are intrinsically connected as one collective story. There should not be an understanding that there is a New Testament and an Old Testament. They are part of the same narrative and story. The narrative story of the Tanakh begins with the four primeval events listed (Creation, Garden of Eden, Flood, and Babel) and four primary patriarchs (Abraham, Isaac, Jacob, Joseph) of Genesis. These stories and events form the foundation of the Tanakh and the future of the Biblical story narrative.

The narrative through the Tanakh then picks up with Israel's enslavement and Exodus, the giving of the law, wandering in the wilderness, the conquest of the promised land, judges, the rise of the Israelite monarchy, and ultimately concludes with Israel's exile and subsequent (partial) return to the land. These stories tell the history and story of the Jewish people from the beginning through the creation of the Temple system and the fall of that Temple.

The story narrative diverges in the New Testament period after the fall of the Temple at the hands of the Romans. The New Testament centers on the messianic figure of Jesus, with the Gospels telling the story of his life, death, and resurrection. The rest of the New Testament tells the story of the spread of the Christian church. There is special attention paid to the incorporation of gentiles (non-Jews) into the nascent church, and this question of the role of Gentiles into the church becomes a contentious hotspot for those in the early church. The New Testament concludes with Revelation's visions of the end when God will establish a utopian kingdom.

The Bible itself from a historical story is subject to many levels of debate by archaeologists and historians. Several archaeologists and historians have observed problems in the historical narratives of the Bible questioning where the Bible was influenced by Mesopotamian, Greek, Roman, and other cultures through the thousands of years in which it developed. The problems of authorship or historical criticism observed in this book do not diminish the authenticity of the Torah. The Bible contains beautiful and powerful literature, regardless of its correspondence with what can be historically established. To understand the Bible, we must also understand the political and religious contexts that had so much influence on its formation. The various books of the Bible were written over a long period of time that included the rise and fall of numerous empires far more powerful than the relatively weak state of Israel, including Egypt, Assyria, Babylonia, Persia, Greece and the Hellenistic kingdoms, and Rome.

Cultural Context

Cultural lenses and understanding play a significant role in the deciphering of the Bible to people and translators. How one understands the Bible now is distinctly related to cultural upbringing.

A person who grew up in Samoa may understand the Bible differently than a person who grew up in Ukraine. To understand the books of the Bible, we must consider the political and religious worlds in which they were produced. Politically, Israel and Judah were dominated by the great empires of the ancient Near East, including Egypt, Assyria (which destroyed Samaria in 722 B.C.E), Babylonia (destroyed Jerusalem in 586 B.C.E.), Persia, Greece/ later Hellenistic kingdoms, and Rome.

As for the religious context, the ancient world featured hundreds of religions with several key features in common. These religions were generally polytheistic, focused on the present life rather than an afterlife, and worshiped powerful deities through cultic acts usually performed in sacred places. Having a diverse and different context in which the ancient world perceived the afterlife influenced and developed very different biblical views of life after death: David did not believe in life after death, while the context of an afterlife appears later after the end of David's life.

In the ancient world, the practices of worshiping deities in diverse and sacred places were a way of accessing and applying the favor of these powerful divine entities. Ancient religions thus lacked the emphasis upon doctrines, ethics, the afterlife, and sacred books that tend to characterize modern (Western) religious traditions. More important, there was no separation between church and state in antiquity. The concept of a separation of church and state is a product of American political philosophy. Instead, national or civic gods were worshiped out of duty and respect. Finally, because ancient religions were polytheistic, they were non-exclusive—worshiping one god in no way meant giving up the worship of other divine beings.

The religion of Israel, which later developed into Judaism, shared many of these characteristics but was distinctive in that it required the exclusive worship of only one God, who had made a special "covenant" or political contract with Israel. Israel's side of the contract required adherence to the Law of Moses. Also, unlike other religions, Judaism ultimately settled on a single sacred site for the cultic worship of this God: a specific temple in Jerusalem. After the destruction of the first Jerusalem temple and the scattering of many Jews across various nations, synagogues arose as places for prayer and teaching. No sacrifices were made in synagogues, however. These uniquely Jewish perspectives were foundational to early Christianity as well. Despite their uniqueness, Judaism and Christianity did paradoxically assimilate many religious ideas and practices from other religions.

Challenges for Studying the Bible

The Bible is a long and complicated collection. There is not a single author in the Bible, nor is the Bible consistent on the language it is written in because of all the different languages that influenced the authorship of the Bible. Its books were written over a long period of time by different authors with diverse audiences, concerns, and perspectives. Even the exact books that comprise the biblical canon are not entirely uniform.

The Bible was also originally written in several different ancient languages. The Jewish scriptures were written almost entirely in Hebrew (with a few sections in the related language of Aramaic). The Hebrew books in the Apocrypha written during the intertestamental period are written in a different form and style of Hebrew than early Paleo Hebrew as well. The New Testament was written in Greek. The Jewish Bible was also transmitted in a Greek translation called the Septuagint (LXX) in antiquity; this version was the primary Bible of many early Jews and was widely used by early Christians.

Many of the early writers of the New Testament may have referenced the Septuagint as a source for their Epistles and Gospels. This is further complicated by the wide span of time covered between the authorship of each text. The diversity of time and composition of books, even those texts written in the same language, are diverse-- consider that Shakespeare's English is dramatically different from modern American English. Koine Greek is different from modern Greek.

The complicated process of translation—especially from ancient tongues to a modern one—ensures that not even the words of the Bible are always exactly agreed upon, let alone the meaning of those words. Translations and meanings are assumed by translators and often can have problems associated with those translations. Idioms, such as the phrase "son of God," also presume a level of shared language and culture, only adding to these difficulties.

The Bible also includes numerous literary genres, each of which has its own implicit rules of communication. One does not read a personal letter, in the same manner, one reads an epic novel, for example. The level of formality in writing varies depending on the skill of the author and the target audience of the writer. The same holds accurate for the Bible: it is important not to read an apocalypse like Revelation in the same way one reads a letter of Paul or a poem in Psalms. Even within the same genre, the Bible contains many internal tensions, as each book has a distinct outlook. Some books address similar concerns from very different—often seemingly contradictory—perspectives.

Understanding context is critically important to properly understand the Bible. Understanding the context is true both in a textual sense and a broader cultural sense.

The various authors of the Bible had quite different cosmological perspectives from modern people—or even sometimes from each other. An eighth-century B.C.E. prophet was not writing about twenty-first-century issues or first-century issues. This does not negate that the writings of then are applicable today.

Misunderstandings are inevitable when these differences are not accounted for in interpretations, and people can misapply the historical Bible incorrectly.

Finally, the biblical texts were passed down through many centuries as handwritten copies. The transmission of biblical texts through the generations led to numerous changes, both intentional and accidental. The transmission of the biblical text with accidental or intentional changes leads to an additional layer of uncertainty when interpreting the Bible. The New Testament's additions and changes in the transmission of the original language do not discount the authority and authenticity of the work-- especially not the importance. It must be taken into account that some things have changed over time.

A Literary and Historical Approach

As a scholar of biblical literature, the readers of this book must approach the literary and historical aspects of the Bible as essential to understanding the context and application of the writings. As an approach to interpreting and applying the Bible to the modern life, the biblical writings must be seen as ancient literature, evaluating the structure of each book and reading carefully while taking into account the flow of the narrative, literary motifs, and the possibility that other sources may have been used by the biblical authors and editors. In the process, each book will be read on its terms, which will sometimes reveal different perspectives among different books of the Bible (and sometimes even within the same book). By reading the Bible in its unique authorship, it provides the biblical reader with a clear insight into the understanding of the Bible.

A second approach must be implemented when reading the Bible, and that is the historical approach. When we take a historical approach, establishing the historical setting (as much as possible) for each book while also assessing how the book corresponds to what we can know from other sources, such as archaeology or accounts external to the Bible, the story and literature become alive for the reader. Some students may find a literary-historical approach at odds with their faith commitments and prior understanding of the Bible. This is normal as it challenges original thought and contributes to the overall growth of a person's faith journey. Nevertheless, one must take the biblical literature seriously on its terms, opening new interpretive possibilities. Books like Job tell a story of pain and suffering. The historical focus should likewise be understood as distinct from a confessional perspective. This book investigates how best to understand the Bible from a literary and historical perspective but will not try to convince anyone either to believe or disbelieve the faith claims of the Bible.

CHAPTER 2

Authorship of the Bible

Challenges for Studying the Bible

The Bible is a long and complicated collection. There is not a single author, nor is the Bible consistent on the language of composition. Its books were written over a long period of time by different authors with different audiences, concerns, and perspectives. Even the exact books that comprise the biblical canon are not entirely uniform.

The Bible was also originally written in several different ancient languages. The Jewish scriptures were written almost entirely in Hebrew (with a few sections in the related language of Aramaic). The Hebrew books in the Apocrypha written during the intertestamental period are written in a different form and style of Hebrew than early Paleo Hebrew as well. The New Testament was written in Greek. The Jewish Bible was also transmitted in a Greek translation called the Septuagint (LXX) in antiquity; this version was the primary

Bible of many early Jews and was widely used by early Christians. Many of the early writers of the New Testament may have referenced the Septuagint as a source for their Epistles and Gospels. This is further complicated by the wide span of time covered by even those texts written in the same language (consider that Shakespeare's English is dramatically different from modern American English). Koine Greek is different from modern Greek. The complicated process of translation—especially from ancient tongues to a modern one—ensures that not even the words of the Bible are always exactly agreed upon, let alone the meaning of those words. Translations and meanings are assumed by translators and often can have problems associated with those translations. Idioms, such as the phrase "son of God," also presume a level of shared language and culture, only adding to these difficulties.

The Bible also includes numerous literary genres, each of which has its own implicit rules of communication. One does not read a personal letter, in the same manner, one reads an epic novel, for example. The level of formality in writing varies depending on the skill of the author and the target audience of the writer. The same holds accurate for the Bible: it is important not to read an apocalypse like Revelation in the same way one reads a letter of Paul or a poem in Psalms. Even within the same genre, the Bible contains many internal tensions, as each book has a distinct outlook. Some books address similar concerns from very different—often seemingly contradictory—perspectives.

Understanding context is critically important to properly understand the Bible. Understanding the context is true both in a textual sense and a broader cultural sense. The various authors of the Bible had quite different cosmological perspectives from modern people—or even sometimes from each other. An eighth-century B.C.E. prophet was not writing about twenty-first-century issues or first-century issues. This does not negate that the writings of then are applicable today.

Misunderstandings are inevitable when dealing with biblical texts.

Finally, the biblical texts were passed down through many centuries as handwritten copies. This led to numerous changes, both intentional and accidental, leading to an additional layer of uncertainty when interpreting the Bible. The New Testament's additions and changes in the transmission of the original language do not discount the authority and authenticity of the work-- especially not the importance. It must be taken into account that some things have changed over time.

A Literary and Historical Approach

As a scholar of biblical literature, the readers of this book must approach the literary and historical aspects of the Bible as essential to understanding the context and application of the writings. As an approach to interpreting and applying the

Bible to the modern life, the biblical writings must be seen as ancient literature, evaluating the structure of each book and reading carefully while taking into account the flow of the narrative, literary motifs, and the possibility that other sources may have been used by the biblical authors and editors. In the process, each book will be read on its terms, which will sometimes reveal different perspectives among different books of the Bible (and sometimes even within the same book). This provides the biblical reader with a clear insight into the understanding of the Bible.

Who Wrote the Pentateuch?

Traditionally, Moses has been regarded as the author of the Pentateuch. Moses is attributed to have received direct revelation from God on Mount Sinai. This perspective has been questioned not only in the modern period but also in the Middle Ages and even earlier. Early readers noticed that the books of the Torah themselves make no claim about their author but are instead anonymous. Moses is the leading character, but he is referred to in the third person rather than the first—suggesting these books are *about* Moses, not *by* him. Similarly, it is difficult to explain how Moses might have written the account of his own death or refer to the rise of the Israelite monarchy (Gen 36:31).

The internal tensions or inconsistencies within the Pentateuch have become especially important for modern scholars. The two creation stories of Genesis, for example, contain several striking differences, such as discrepancies on whether humanity was created before or after animals or plants or whether male and female were created at the same time (Gen 1:26–27) or male first and female sometime later (Gen 2). The deity is also called by different names in the two creation narratives: *Elohim* (=God) in Gen 1 and *YHWH Elohim*, featuring the personal name of the God of Israel (YHWH), in the second story. Moreover, the deity is portrayed in more anthropomorphic terms in the second story, while the first story depicts God as more distant and remote. The stories also appear to have different interests, with the first stressing the Sabbath and the second looking more at explaining the origins of specific aspects of human life.

The flood story (Gen 6–9) provides another striking example: Did Noah take two animals of every kind into the Ark (Gen 6:19) or seven pairs of clean animals and two of every other kind of animal (Gen 7:2)? One particularly striking example is the statement in Exodus 6:3 that prior to the revelation to Moses, God had not revealed Himself to the patriarchs by the personal name YHWH. At the same time, Genesis 4:26 says, "At that time people began to invoke the name of YHWH," and Genesis 15:6–8 tells of God revealing himself to Abraham by the name YHWH.

The Documentary Hypothesis

Most modern scholars have concluded that these tensions reflect different sources spliced together by a later editor. The traditional scholarly model is called the Documentary Hypothesis, most closely associated with German scholar Julius Wellhausen (1844–1918). This model suggests that there were, in fact, four distinct Pentateuchal sources from different authors living at different times. These sources are usually referred to by their initials, which is why this model is often known as the JEDP hypothesis.

The J (Jahwist) source is named for its preferred use of the divine name YHWH (=Yahweh, Jahweh in German), while the E (Elohist) and P (Priestly) sources prefer the name Elohim (=God). The J source is known for especially anthropomorphic depictions of the deity and concern with the southern part of Israel (i.e., Judah). The E source is much more fragmentary, with many scholars arguing that J and E are not separate sources, and focuses on the northern part of Israel. The P source is notable for its concerns with priestly issues such as sacrifice, purity laws, genealogies, and so on. The D source is limited to the book of Deuteronomy and is thought to date to the time of Josiah, the king of Judah, or perhaps slightly earlier.

Scholarly opinion about Pentateuchal sources is now quite varied and typically departs significantly from the traditional JEDP model, though scholars are agreed that the Pentateuch was not written by Moses but is instead the result of a variety of written sources from different times and with different concerns.

Oral Traditions and Cultural Parallels

These written sources were derived from much older oral traditions that had been told and retold for generations. Numerous parallels from Israel's surrounding cultures have also been discovered over the last few centuries, including creation stories like the *Enuma Elish* and flood stories like the *Gilgamesh Epic*. Parallels from these two stories, in particular, are too striking to be accidental: Genesis seems to have borrowed heavily from its neighbors.

A second approach must be implemented when reading the Bible, and that is the historical approach. When we take a historical approach, establishing the historical setting (as much as possible) for each book while also assessing how the book corresponds to what we can know from other sources, such as archaeology or accounts external to the Bible, the story and literature become alive for the reader. Some students may find a literary-historical approach at odds with their faith commitments and prior understanding of the Bible. This is normal as it challenges original thought and contributes to the overall growth of a person's faith journey. Nevertheless, one must take the biblical literature seriously on its terms, opening new interpretive possibilities. Books like Job tell a story of pain and suffering. The historical focus should likewise be understood as distinct from a confessional perspective. This book investigates how best to understand the Bible from a literary and historical perspective but will not try to convince anyone either to believe or disbelieve the faith claims of the Bible.

The Canon of the Hebrew Bible

The word "canon" means "measuring rod" and came to refer to a rule or standard by which something could be judged. Modern scholars think the five-book collection of the Torah was canonical by the fifth-century B.C.E. (partly on the testimony of the book of Ezra) and the Nevi'im (both the Former and Latter Prophets) by the second-century B.C.E. Part of the reason for the latter is that some books that might otherwise have been included in this collection (like Daniel) are not—likely because they were written after the collection became fixed. The Kethuvim were debated over a longer period, and the books included in this group were somewhat fluid, but most scholars think they were largely agreed upon by about the time of the destruction of the second Temple in 70 C.E. These decisions seem to have relied on three criteria: (i) language (only books written in Hebrew or primarily in Hebrew), (ii) age (must be from before the fourth century or attributed to an author living before that time), and (iii) usage (those most widely and frequently used).

The Canon of the New Testament

We are better informed about the process of New Testament canonization as we have records of church fathers explicitly discussing the matter. The earliest Christians were, of course, Jews, and therefore inherited the Jewish scriptures. But in the process of self-differentiation, the lines between orthodoxy and heresy needed to be defined. Numerous pseudonymous books also laid claim to authority, which also contributed to the need for declaring which books were authoritative. The "orthodox" church fathers who decided the canon applied four main criteria: (i) antiquity (must go back to the beginning of Christianity), (ii) apostolicity (must be written by or ascribed to an apostle or his associate), (iii) catholicity (universally used throughout the church), and (iv) orthodoxy (must agree with the orthodox theology of those making the decisions).

Apparently, the first person to put a Christian canon together was Marcion, whose canon included the letters of Paul and a version of the Gospel of Luke. Marcion's opponents claimed Marcion had eliminated properly authoritative books, which helped provide the impetus for deciding which were authoritative. The first known list of all twenty-seven books of the New Testament comes from a letter from Athanasius, the bishop of Alexandria, Egypt, in 367 c.e.

The Text of the Hebrew Bible

Ancient texts were copied by hand; the term "manuscript" literally means "handwritten copy." These texts were passed down as handwritten copies until the invention of the printing press in the fifteenth-century C.E. This meant that the scribes who copied these texts by hand could—and did—change the texts they were copying, either on purpose or by accident.

The oldest complete copy of the Hebrew Bible is Codex Leningradensis, which comes from around 1000 C.E. Part of the reason we don't have older copies is that it appears that Jewish scribes from the Middle Ages destroyed the manuscripts they used to make their copies once their own copies were complete. All modern translations today are based on this codex, which is part of the Masoretic Text tradition, handed down by scholars who devised strict scribal rules for preserving biblical traditions between 500 and 1000 C.E. The Masoretes standardized the entire consonantal text of the Hebrew Bible and also devised a system of dots and dashes added around the consonants to indicate the appropriate vowels for each word (ancient Hebrew was not written with vowels). Most scholars today have concluded that the consonants of the Masoretic Text were already largely fixed by the end of the first-century C.E.

The discovery of the Dead Sea Scrolls, however, provided manuscripts of the Hebrew Bible over one thousand years older than Codex Leningradensis. These Scrolls did not, however, include complete manuscripts of the entire Hebrew Bible. In many instances, the text of the Scrolls is very similar to the Masoretic Text. In other cases, however, the texts from the Scrolls are quite different from the Masoretic Text, such as in Samuel, Kings, and one of the copies of Jeremiah (which is more similar to the Septuagint's version of Jeremiah). These differences suggest that the text of the Hebrew Bible was more fluid before the first-century C.E.

CHAPTER 3

The New Testament

The Manuscripts of the New Testament

We do not have the original copies ("autographs") of any early Christian writings; over time, the original copies wore out, were lost, or were destroyed. Instead, we possess copies of copies of copies that were produced hundreds of years after the original authors wrote the original texts. The individuals who copied these texts often were not trained scribes, introducing errors into the writings—and even professional copyists made mistakes. Once a mistake entered into a text, the next scribe typically copied that mistake and added others.

Our earliest manuscripts of Paul's letters and full copies of the Gospels date to around the early third century (though we have fragments of manuscripts from somewhat earlier). The earliest full manuscripts of the entire New Testament date to around the fourth century. We currently possess around 5,700 manuscripts—from fragments to full texts—that date between the second and fifteenth centuries. Although we have far more copies of the New Testament than of any other ancient book, we still cannot be completely certain about the original words of these texts, because no two of these copies are exactly alike. Scholars of textual criticism, however, suggest that if we understand the types of changes that were introduced into the texts, we can come close to recovering the words of the New Testament authors.

Changes in the New Testament Text

Most mistakes in these manuscripts were unintentional mistakes (e.g., misspelled words; omitted words, verses, or pages; rearranged words; added words or verses) that were made because ancient writings did not contain punctuation, paragraph divisions, or spaces between words (verse divisions did not even exist until 1551). These types of changes are easily recognized. Sometimes, though, scribes intentionally changed the text. These modifications are more challenging for scholars to identify. Some of these changes may have been made because a scribe wished to correct historical information or grammatical errors present in the text. Other times, scribes "harmonized" one text to another. Finally, some changes appear to reflect Christian doctrine. A text that sounded Gnostic or adoptionistic might have been changed to sound more "orthodox."

Criteria for Establishing the Original Text

Textual criticism seeks to establish the original text by testing a passage against a number of criteria:

1. *Age of the Manuscripts.* The form of a text that is supported by the oldest manuscript is more likely to reflect the original words.

2. *Distribution of the Manuscripts.* If a particular reading is prevalent in one geographic area and is different from a reading that is widespread, it is likely that the first is a local variation.

3. *Considerations of Style.* With this criterion, scholars concentrate on an author's, not a scribe's, tendencies. Passages that contain vocabulary, grammatical constructions, or theology that differs from that in the rest of the book are likely scribal changes.

4. *The More Difficult Reading.* Scholars suggest that the more difficult reading is likely to be closer to the original, since scribes were more likely to make a passage easier than harder to understand.

5. *Quality of the Manuscripts.* If a manuscript is full of errors, then readings within that manuscript must be regarded with suspicion.

Perhaps surprisingly to most new to the discipline, the number of manuscripts that have a particular reading is not especially important, since many of those copies may derive from a late manuscript (one that may contain more mistakes) while only a few may derive from an earlier one, which has presumably undergone fewer revisions.

The Original Text of the New Testament

This chapter shows that we cannot rely on inherited texts to perfectly reflect an author's exact words, since the manuscripts contain changes and mistakes. Scholars, then, must weigh each reading against the criteria discussed previously in order to reconstruct the best possible approximation of the "original text."

The Text of the New Testament

The New Testament contains twenty-seven books written in Greek by fifteen or sixteen different authors. They were written to communities or individuals between the years 50 and 120 C.E. The Gospels, which are biographies of Jesus, are traditionally attributed to disciples (Matthew and John) and associates of the apostles (Mark and Luke). The book of Acts, written by the author of the Gospel of Luke, narrates the spread of Christianity through the Roman Empire. Next are twenty-one epistles written by various authors to particular individuals or communities addressing issues of belief, practice, and ethics. Thirteen of these letters claim to be written by Paul. The last book of the New Testament, Revelation, is an apocalypse. This book describes the course of events leading to the destruction of the world and the coming of the new Kingdom of God.

We know of other early Christian writings not included in the New Testament. In 1 Corinthians, for instance, Paul says that he previously sent a letter to the church at Corinth. Unfortunately, this correspondence is no longer extant. There are, in addition, other noncanonical, proto-orthodox writings that have survived. Most important, perhaps, is the collection of second-century writings by authors referred to as the "Apostolic Fathers." Some of these books were considered authoritative in many churches. In addition to proto-orthodox texts, we have Gnostic texts from the Nag Hammadi library and a variety of other early Gospels, histories, epistles, and apocalypses.

The first Christians were Jewish, and their authoritative text was the Hebrew Bible. Near the end of the first century, however, Christians began to place Jesus' sayings on a par with Scripture (1 Tim 5:18). Although Paul seems to have thought of himself as an authoritative spokesperson for the true gospel, he did not think of his correspondence as Scripture. The author of 2 Peter, however, included Paul's letters among the Scriptures (2 Pet 3:16). Marcion seems to have been the first to compile a Christian canon, and Marcion's collection (and the conflict surrounding it) evidently led other Christians to create their own sets of authoritative texts. Proto-orthodox Christianity did not immediately develop a closed canon of

Scripture; on the contrary, it was not until 367 C.E. that the present twenty-seven books of the New Testament were listed as an authoritative canon. Up to and during this time, proto-orthodox Christians continued to debate which books belonged in the canon, with the arguments centering upon three primary criteria: the books had to be ancient, they had to be thought to have been written by an apostle (or close associate), and they had to be accepted among proto-orthodox congregations as reflecting orthodox belief.

We have an abundance of ancient manuscripts of the New Testament, some of them from as early as the second century. Still, these were not subjected to the rigorous control guiding the Medieval scribes of the Hebrew Bible. There are numerous variant readings—differences in wording among manuscripts. Most of these are insignificant, such as spelling errors. Some, however, do matter, including intentional changes. Scribes sometimes changed texts to say what they thought it *should* say, and these changes would be propagated by the next scribe using that altered manuscript. The longer ending of Mark and the story of Jesus and the woman taken in adultery from John 7:53–8:11 are two examples of later insertions into texts that did not originally include these passages. Although the modern discipline of textual criticism can help determine which are most likely the earliest readings, we cannot be 100 percent sure that we have the original words the New Testament authors wrote.

CHAPTER 4

Who is Jesus

The World of Jesus and His Followers

For purposes of this book, the divinity of Jesus will not be addressed-- this book will look at the Historical figure of Jesus. Jesus was a prolific and history-altering person.

The story of this teacher (some call Rabbi now) begins in the New Testament. As with the Tanakh, teaching or studying the New Testament is complicated by the difference between modern and ancient worldviews. Our modern views of theology are through a lens of culture, time, and religious ideology.

Protestantism, the Western Church, and the Eastern Church have different views regarding the role of Jesus within a person's life. From a historical perspective, to understand the stories in the New Testament, readers must first familiarize themselves with the culture, society, and assumptions of the Greco-Roman world. Greece and Rome had different laws, views, and customs than a modern human. To understand the stories about Jesus, they must be placed in their first-century context to understand how first-century pagans and Jews make sense of these stories? The parables, the stories, and the dating of these stories make an impact on how a story is read in the New Testament.

The History of the Greco-Roman World

The term "Greco-Roman world" designates the lands surrounding the Mediterranean from the time of Alexander the Great (356–323 B.C.E.) through the first three or four centuries of the Roman Empire. Alexander the Great spread Greek language and culture ("Hellenization") throughout his empire. The Roman Empire arose in the context of the Hellenistic world; it took advantage of the cultural unity of language and custom established through Hellenization. The Roman Empire was massive, and after the civil war that resulted in Octavian/Augustus becoming emperor, there was a nearly two hundred year period of relative peace and security (the "Pax Romana" or "Roman Peace") across the empire. A common language (mostly Greek), standard coinage, fantastic roads, and stable governance made travel possible.

The stories of Jesus are similar to other stories of peace told in Greek history. Traditions about the life of a first-century neo-Pythagorean teacher, Apollonius of Tyana, closely parallel traditions about Jesus. The similarities reveal that Jesus is one of many reputed miracle-working

Sons of God in antiquity. The question then becomes, why did he become revered and written about person?

In the context of the Roman and Greek worlds, Jesus is juxtaposed to Polytheism. Polytheism remained the norm in the culture and time in which Jesus was emerging. There were also no empire-wide organizations that oversaw the worship of the gods. Creedal statements were unnecessary because it was not belief, but cultic acts of worship, such as animal sacrifice, that pleased the gods. Moreover, ethical demands played a minimal role in religiosity. Also, the afterlife was of little concern to most residents of the empire. Worship of the gods centered on day-to-day survival and was not focused on an otherworldly existence. There was also no separation between church and state. The gods, contingent on proper worship, protected the empire, and the state, in turn, promoted the proper care of the gods (cultus deorum). Finally, tolerance of a range of religious beliefs and practices was a central aspect of the Greco-Roman religion.

Many Romans seem to have believed in a divine pyramid of sorts, with one supreme god (Zeus, Jupiter, or an unknowable god) at the top. Below this one God was the great gods of the ancient Mediterranean world: Poseidon, Hera, Aphrodite, Artemis, and others. The next tier of divine beings was the daimonia, a group of lesser deities who had limited power but who were in direct contact with humans. Included in this group were deities of particular villages, towns, or families. The gap between divine beings and humans was bridged by great men, philosophers, or warriors whose lives had been so extraordinary that at their deaths, the gods made them immortal. Related to this last group were demigods, individuals born from the union of a mortal and a god. Because stories of supernatural births and familial ties to the gods were more or less commonplace in stories of extraordinary men, the story of Jesus as God's son would not have been incomprehensible to an ancient audience.

Judaism in the Times of Jesus

Judaism was one of the religions of the Greco-Roman world, and it is perhaps most important for our study because Jesus and his earliest followers were Jews. Jesus was an astute teacher of Torah. The followers of Jesus read Jewish scriptures, worshiped the Jewish God, and kept Jewish customs. The Jewish most likely observed Kosher laws. There were millions of Jews outside of Israel as well in Greece and in Egypt. To understand Jesus, then, we must first understand first-century Judaism.

Approximately 7 percent of the Roman Empire (about four million people) were Jews. Most of these Jews did not live in Israel; after the Babylonian captivity, many Jews did not return to the land but instead remained where they had settled, places like Babylon or Egypt. Others traveled and settled elsewhere. This dispersion of the Jews from Israel is known as the Diaspora, and most Jews of the Roman Diaspora spoke Greek, not Hebrew. Jews were distinctive in the ancient world in that those who set-tled in new lands continued to retain their native customs and religion rather than merely adopting the customs and religions of their new locations.

These Jews continued to worship only the God of Israel, circumcise their boys, and follow kosher food laws. Since the sacrificial worship of the Jewish God took place exclusively in Jerusalem, at the only Temple for the God of Israel, most Jews could not worship in the Jerusalem Temple. As a result, synagogues, houses of prayer and study, arose. Although Jews were quite diverse, almost all Jews continued to share the characteristics of monotheism, the covenant, and commitment to the Torah. Jews were unique among ancient groups in having "scriptures," though the full Tanakh was not yet fully defined or agreed upon.

The Romans had been in control of Israel since the Roman general Pompey's defeat of the Hasmoneans in 63 B.C.E. and remained so throughout the New Testament period. The land itself was divided into three regions. Judea was in the south with basically the same territory as the historical southern kingdom of Judah. North of Judea was the region of Samaria, inhabited by Samari-tans, despised "half-breeds" descended from northern Israelites (not "Jews," since they were not from Judah) and those resettled in the area by Assyria centuries earlier. Galilee was in the far north and was a mostly rural area mostly inhabited by Jews. The Romans generally avoided direct rule but instead governed through oversight of local aristocrats put in charge as "clients" of Rome. So long as there were no rebellions and tax revenues came in, everything was fine. When Jesus was born, a client king, Herod the Great (who was famous for his great building projects, including a major renovation of the Temple), ruled all of Palestine. By the time Jesus was an adult, Galilee was ruled by Herod's son, Herod Antipas, but Judea was ruled by the Roman governor Pontius Pilate, though the high priest in Jerusalem served as the de facto day-to-day ruler, reporting to Pilate on essential matters. Aramaic was the primary language of the land, though the better educated also spoke Greek.

The prominent Jewish historian, Josephus, described four philosophies (or groups) of Judaism that arose around the time of the Maccabean revolt: Pharisees, Sadducees, Essenes, and the Fourth Philosophy.

The Pharisees were a group of devout Jews who were, above all else, intent on keeping the Law in its entirety. Since the laws given to Moses were often vague, the Pharisees debated what was and was not allowed if one was to keep the laws (these decisions are known as the "oral law"; the written form of these oral traditions is known as the Mishnah, the heart of the Talmud). The Pharisees held very little political power until after the Jewish revolt against Rome that culminated in the destruction of the Temple in 70 C.E.

The Sadducees were the political players in Jesus' lifetime. They were the priestly and aristocratic Jews whose primary affiliation was with the Jerusalem Temple. They also made up the majority of the Sanhedrin, the local Jewish council. They did not subscribe to the Pharisaic oral laws or believe in an afterlife (as opposed to the Pharisees). They deemed authoritative only the five books of Moses (the Pentateuch).

The Essenes were a separatist group that believed that the Pharisees were too lax in their religious observances and that the Sadducees were corrupt and had defiled the Temple (mainly because a non-Zadokite high priest was appointed by the Hasmoneans). Some Essenes left Jerusalem and settled in the desert near the Dead Sea. In 1947, a collection of their texts was discovered, known as the Dead Sea Scrolls. In addition to stringent community rules and several other kinds of texts, these scrolls contain portions of all the books of the Hebrew Bible except Esther. The Essenes are the only one of the four philosophies not mentioned in the New Testament.

The Fourth Philosophy referred to a number of individual groups whose common goal was to overthrow the foreign powers that ruled the land of Israel. These groups favored armed rebellion against foreign authorities. Among the groups were the Sicarii (the "daggermen") and the Zealots.

Putting the New Testament and Early Christianity on the Map

Jesus is thought to have been born around 4 B.C.E. and died around 30 C.E. The four gospels record his ministry and death. Acts tells the story of the growth of the early church through its first thirty years or so, focusing on the ministry of the apostle Paul. The rest of the New Testament contains thirteen letters (allegedly) written by Paul to various churches and individuals, eight other letters, and one apocalypse (Revelation). Paul's writings are the earliest New Testament documents, but we will start with the Gospels since those letters presume knowledge of Jesus.

To reconstruct the past, historians would prefer numerous corroborating, internally consistent, and disinterested independent sources from as near the time to the event itself as possible. Unfortunately, Jesus is not mentioned by any pagan writer from the first century. Tacitus, a Roman historian writing around 115 C.E., provides the first historical information from pagan literature about Jesus' life, and he only mentions that Pontius Pilate executed Jesus. Only one non-Christian Jewish source from the first century mentions Jesus. Josephus's Antiquities of the Jews briefly reports that Jesus was a teacher and a "doer of startling deeds," who had Jewish and Gentile followers and was condemned to the cross by Pilate.

Since the non-Christian sources give us little helpful information, we must rely on (biased) Christian texts. As we have seen, the noncanonical Gospels are late and usually rely on earlier materials. Thus, they are of little use to historians seeking the historical Jesus. One might expect that Paul, the earliest New Testament author, would be a good source of information about the historical Jesus, but, Paul says rather little about Jesus' life. Thus, historians are primarily limited to the New Testament Gospels for information about the historical Jesus.

Jesus the Apocalyptic Prophet

Many of the earliest sources we have for Jesus' life depict him as a Jewish apocalypticist. Jesus talked much of a time to come in the future and the Kingdom of God. As such, he proclaimed that Jews must repent and return to God in the face of the imminent end of the present age, which would entail the judgment of the world by the Son of Man, the destruction of evil, and the coming of the Kingdom of God. The earliest sources for Jesus' life, teachings, and death (Mark, Q, M, and L) show him as an apocalypticist. These sources, moreover, are independent of one another. Many of the stories that show Jesus as an apocalypticist pass the criterion of dissimilarity, and all of them are contextually credible (we have already seen that apocalypticism was a part of several Jewish sects).

Perhaps the most compelling reason to view Jesus as an apocalyptic prophet is the line of apocalypticism that precedes and follows him. Jesus associated with John the Baptist, whose ministry was apocalyptic, and we know that the earliest Christian churches were apocalyptic. The only connection between John and the later Christian community is Jesus. Jesus' apocalypticism, first influenced by John the Baptist, must have been the source of apocalypticism in the early church.

Many Jesus' sayings refer to the imminent arrival of the Son of Man, the approaching Day of Judgment, the importance of repentance and preparation, and the coming Kingdom of God. Taking into account the criterion of dissimilarity (the Gospel writers are ambiguous about Jesus referring to himself as the Son of Man), some scholars think Jesus did not equate himself with the cosmic Son of Man, but instead expected that this figure from Daniel 7 would soon come to judge the world. Furthermore, Jesus' ethical teachings—especially his emphasis that God will ultimately make things right—coincide with his apocalyptic worldview.

Christian descriptions of events leading up to Jesus' crucifixion also contribute to a portrayal of Jesus as an apocalypticist. If Jesus had been just a Jewish reformer, there would have been little reason for Roman authorities to notice him. If his message was subversive—that is, if he prophesied the downfall of the present regime and the coming of a new kingdom—there would indeed be a reason to kill him.

Jesus took his apocalyptic message to the heart of Judaism—to the Jerusalem Temple—during Passover, a time when a large number of Jews were available to hear his teachings, when Jesus entered the Temple and wreaked havoc, denouncing the Temple authorities and predicting the destruction of the Temple.

At Jesus' last supper with the disciples, he interpreted his death as bringing forgiveness of sins. Although this was a Christian teaching and thus did not pass the criterion of dissimilarity, it does show the apocalyptic implications of Jesus' death and is reflected in two early independent sources. It is likely that Jesus anticipated Jewish reaction to his teachings and was not surprised when he was arrested. He was betrayed by Judas, tried, and crucified for calling himself king of the Jews.

CHAPTER 5

Historically Matthew

The Gospel of Matthew

The book of Matthew, known as the Gospel of Matthew, used a variety of authorship sources to refer and copy. The author of the Gospel of Matthew used Mark (Gospel of Mark), Q, and the author's own sources (designated by scholars as "M"). The Gospel was written between 80–85 C.E., and as late as 105 C.E., probably somewhere outside of Israel. Dating Matthew is critical to understand because it is viewed as the most Jewish of the Gospel accounts; however, it would have been written after the book of Acts.

Matthew's Jesus is unmistakably Jewish; the genealogy in the first chapter emphasizes Jesus' connection to two of the most influential figures in Jewish history, David and Abraham. Matthew adds an account of Jesus' birth that does not appear in Mark. Matthew's emphasis on Jesus' Jewish roots and the insistence that his life was a fulfillment of prophecy can be traced from the genealogy to the birth narrative and through the rest of the Gospel. A portrait and image of Jesus as a Jewish man who was influential in his region is conveyed by the author of Matthew. Matthew uses "fulfillment citations" in the writing of Matthew to show a connection and bridge between the Tanakh and the entire Hebrew Bible with the New Testament to prove that Jesus was the Jewish Messiah and not a prophet. Matthew further emphasizes Jesus' importance to Judaism by modeling his birth and ministry on Moses' birth and mission, a form of literary parallel that is common in Second Temple writing. The dichotomy was presented to show Jesus as the new Moses, who has been appointed by God to free his people from bondage. According to Matthew, people do not need to choose between Jesus and Moses, nor must they choose between Jesus' Law and Moses' Law. Jesus is, for this author, the final interpreter of Mosaic Law and that Jesus is a continuation of Moses' authority.

Jesus teaches much more in Matthew than in Mark. The Sermon on the Mount is the first of five blocks of teaching in Matthew. Much of the Sermon on the Mount comes from Q. This sourcing means that a primary source influenced Matthew, and we don't know what that source was. Since the Q passages are scattered in Luke's Gospel, it appears that Matthew arranged this material into a singular sermon. The five-fold structure may mimic the five books of Moses. This sermon is a clear example of

Matthew's propensity to equate Moses' and Jesus' roles: Jesus delivers the Law of God while standing on a mountain. The Sermon deals mainly with life in the kingdom of heaven, an earthly kingdom that God will establish on earth. The Beatitudes serve as assurances to those who are currently weak and oppressed—they will have a place in the kingdom of heaven. The Beatitudes do not, therefore, are not commands but statements of fact. These statements attest to the state of being a person who is in a relationship with God.

In the Gospel, according to the book of Matthew, Jesus does not advocate abandoning the Mosaic Law. The Mosaic Law is to be lived to the 'fullest' and not done away with. Jesus insists he has not come to abolish the Law but to fulfill it, which means he is actually keeping the law the best he is capable of doing. Jesus urges his followers to keep the Law even more rigorously than the scribes and Pharisees, and affirms that the law continues even in his believer's actions. Jesus explains what he means in the passages of the Sermon on the Mount, known as the "antitheses." In these statements, it is clear that God's people are called to keep not just the letter but the spirit of the Law. It is a total commitment to God.

In the Sermon on the Mount, the Law is summarized in two commandments: "Love the Lord your God with all your heart, and with all your soul, and with all your mind" and "Love your neighbor as yourself." This command written by Matthew and attributed to Jesus is an affirmation of the liturgical prayer said by Jews daily called, the Shema. Thus, love is at the core of the entire Law and is reflected in the ministry of Jesus as a continuation of Moses.

Jesus is presented as thoroughly Jewish in the Gospel of Matthew; however, he strongly opposes a certain sect of Judaism as it is practiced by the leaders of his day in a manner that is unauthentic. Jesus never abolishes the Law and Jesus even requires Jews to keep the Law. For this author of Matthew, the Jewish authorities are hypocrites who are blind to Jesus' messianic identity and the broader view that the Law is, in essence, the love of God. The author typifies and vilified the Jewish leaders in the Passion story. In a story unique to Matthew, Pilate washes his hands of Jesus' blood, and the crowd of Jews cries out, "His blood be on us and on our children" (27:25). Rather than implicating the Jews as a whole for Jesus' death, however, Matthew indicts the Jewish leaders who stir up the crowds; it is the leaders who are responsible for Jesus' death. Unlike Mark, Jesus appears to his disciples at the end of Matthew, with Jesus commanding the disciples to baptize the nations—a commandment that importantly does not distinguish Jews from gentiles.

CHAPTER 6

Book of John: An Exploration of Grace and Love

The Gospel of John

To understand the Gospel of John in the context of love and grace within a historical context is unique because the Gospel of John is considered the most antisemitic of the Gospels in terms of translation. The perceived anti-semitic view of John is opposed to the Gospel of Matthew, which is considered Jewish. The Gospel of John, like the Synoptic Gospels, is a Greco-Roman biography. The context and historical setting of this book originated in the Greco-Roman background and must involve an interpretation of an author who is transmitting a historical story from the Greco-Roman understanding of the Second Temple era.

An examination of the Gospel of John begins with a discussion of the concepts of the transcendence of God.

In the Prologue (John 1:1–18), John reflects on the Logos (typically translated "Word") of God who existed with God from the beginning and who is God. It is only at the end of this mystical reflection that John explains that the Word of God is Jesus. John tells a story of love and grace compared with Logos. The prologue, then, provides the reader with a very different expression of the nature of Jesus than any of the Synoptic Gospels. This biography is not about a mortal man; it is about a being who is, in his own right, divine. The author of the Gospel of John introduces to the reader a concept that Jesus is divine, and the purpose is to hold him or elevate him above a prophet status.

The Gospel of John can be divided into two major parts. The first twelve chapters of the Gospel of John narrate Jesus' public ministry over several years. The stories of Jesus during this time show Jesus connecting with the people. For example, Jesus performs seven public "signs" and gives speeches that demonstrate his identity. Because the author of Matthew speaks of Jesus as divine, Jesus has clearly expressed his identity. The result by Jesus is that he condemns those who do not believe and eventually decides to end his public ministry.

In the second half of the Gospel of John, the next seven chapters (13–19) take place over the course of only one day. The author of the Gospel of Matthew enters depicts how Jesus has his last supper with his disciples and is betrayed. He delivers a final speech, known as the

Farewell Address, in which he explains that he will soon return to heaven, but he will send the Holy Spirit to the disciples for assistance and comfort. Chapters 18–21 describe Jesus' passion and resurrection. John includes a great deal of unique material and does not include many of the Synoptic's most famous stories, such as the virgin birth, Jesus' baptism, the temptation in the wilderness, exorcisms, parables, the transfiguration, or the institution of the Lord's Supper.

Since the book of John does not share the similar stories of the other Gospels, there is a different story told about the love and grace of Jesus being divine that does not seek to validate Jesus' birth, baptism, and other parables of faith. Many scholars, therefore, think John most likely did not use the Synoptic Gospels. Most scholars agree that three of John's unique sources can be isolated on the basis of writing style, repetition of stories, and the presence of literary seams. These sources are the signs source, the Discourse Source, and the Passion Source. John probably used other sources as well (e.g., the prologue and the last chapter of the Gospel). These sources seem to have had their own unique emphases, with some sources presenting Jesus in exalted terms and others portraying Jesus as a mortal human being. Many scholars believe John's community started out with a Synoptic-like understanding of Jesus but eventually came to view him in much higher, exalted terms, a view reflected in the final version of the Gospel of John.

CHAPTER 7

Wisdom Literature vs. Apocalyptic

Wisdom Literature vs. Apocalyptic Literature

Introduction to the Wisdom Literature

Wisdom literature in the Bible are those books that focus on understanding the world and how best to live in it based on an intelligent assessment of life rather than on divine revelation to Israel. While the historical and prophetic books of the Hebrew Bible focus on the historical activities of God, especially with relation to his covenant(s) with Israel, and the concerns of Israel, wisdom literature lacks this subject matter. In contrast, wisdom literature focuses on universal (rather than national) needs, desires, and lives; observation rather than revelation; individual rather than communal focus; and are not uniquely Israelite.

Proverbs

A proverb is by definition a pithy, profound saying encapsulating a unique understanding of the world and/or how best to live in it. Aptly named, the book of Proverbs is a collection of wise sayings to guide life and is thus an example of "positive wisdom," which attempts to explain the order of the world and how people should live. The implication throughout is that some ways of living are better than others—and those who live the right way will prosper for it. Proverbs tends to assume a rather straightforward cause-and-effect mechanism for the world by which people get what they deserve.

The book is divided into three main sections. The first nine chapters contain several wisdom poems and introduce two opposing figures: "Woman Wisdom" and "Strange Woman." The next twenty chapters are simply collections of one pithy saying after another. Chapter 31 ends the book with advice giving by the mother of the otherwise unknown King Lemuel and with an acrostic poem celebrating the ideal wife.

Job

Job is an example of "skeptical wisdom," which observes that the world does not always work out so neatly as positive wisdom might suggest. Sometimes a wise and righteous life is not rewarded; in fact, sometimes the righteous suffer rather severely indeed. Such is the subject matter of

Job, which tells the story of a righteous man who suffers horribly.

Many scholars have concluded that Job is a composite work, with the beginning and end of the book (Job 1–2; 42:7–17) by a different author than the extensive middle portion. The beginning and end are prose narratives, while the middle is a poetic dialogue; the sections prefer different names for the deity; and most importantly, the portrayal of Job and view of suffering is different in each section. The short story is unambiguous about the purpose of Job's suffering: God is testing him, seeing if his righteousness and faithfulness are truly disinterested or whether he is driven by selfish motives. However, the poetic section leaves Job's suffering a mystery, only concluding that God can do what he pleases.

Job's "friends" in the poetic dialogue take a positive wisdom approach in asserting that he must somehow be at fault for the calamity that has come upon him—after all, that is the way the world works! However, Job (and the reader) knows better, and Job demands an audience with God to plead his case. Upon receiving his request, God rebukes him not by giving him an answer for his suffering but by proclaiming his superiority. To this, Job retreats, repentant for questioning that which he could not understand. Taken on its own, the poetic section leaves several interpretive options for an explanation of the problem of suffering, none of which seem to correspond with other views in the Bible, leaving readers (and Job) with many unanswered questions. The prose frame goes on to resolve these questions, though the newly re-enriched Job is still bereaved of his ten original children.

Ecclesiastes

Another example of skeptical wisdom, Ecclesiastes questions the very coherence and logic of the world. The book implies that the author ("Qoheleth," which means "teacher" or perhaps "assembler") is Solomon, claiming to be the "king in Jerusalem" (1:1), fantastically wealthy, and exceedingly wise. However, the language and philosophical traditions of the book far postdate Solomon's life, suggesting a fourth or third century B.C.E. date for the book.

The necessary refrain of the book is that everything under the sun is hevel, a Hebrew word referring to something light, transient, or insignificant. Despite his vast wealth and deeds, the author asserts that nothing done under the sun has lasting consequence or meaning because death brings an end to everything. The principles of positive wisdom are regularly violated in this world, and there is no assurance in the next. The author concludes that the best solution is not to despair but instead to make the most of the time one has. The book itself concludes with the injunction that the only thing that truly matters is to "fear God and keep his commands"—a conclusion that has been called into question by many scholars as out of keeping with the rest of the book. The textbook sides with those scholars who believe this conclusion to be a later editorial addition out of keeping with the opinion of Qoheleth himself.

Apocalyptic Literature

Apocalyptic literature developed out of the prophetic tradition but presented a different perspective from that typically witnessed in the prophets. The term "apocalypticism" comes from the Greek word apocalypsis, which means "uncovering," "unveiling," or "revelation." Jewish apocalypticists believed that God had revealed heavenly secrets to them that could make sense of earthly realities.

The prophets typically linked impending suffering with the people's behavior: they would soon be punished for their sins, and if they turned back to God, they would be restored. Apocalyptic literature, however, addresses the problem of righteous people suffering not because of their sin but because they are righteous. The years leading up to the Maccabean Revolt, for example, offered numerous examples of people being persecuted for following the Torah. Apocalypticism offers another explanation for this state of affairs: Evil supernatural powers are presently in control of this world, opposing God and his people, but God will ultimately intervene and bring justice to the world, destroying his enemies and exalting his people. There are four major tenets of apocalypticism: dualism (opposing forces of light and darkness), pessimism about the present state of this world, belief in the ultimate vindication of God's people, and imminence.

While there are many apocalyptic views, the term "apocalypse" refers to a specific literary genre. Although Jewish and Christian apocalypses differ because of doctrinal differences in the religions, both reflect the beliefs of communities that are experiencing suffering. These books assert that despite present circumstances, God is in charge and will soon intervene and vindicate his people. Apocalypses, then, offer encouragement and assurance to their audiences. In general, writings of this genre share the following features: They are first-person narratives, their highly symbolic visions are interpreted for the prophet by a heavenly being, and the visions involve a triumphal movement from the present suffering of God's people to future vindication and bliss. The two major types of apocalypses are heavenly journeys and historical sketches. These are not mutually exclusive categories; some apocalypses contain both.

Apocalypses also utilize several specific literary features. First, they are typically pseudonymous. Like other pseudonymous works, these texts seek to gain authority by attributing their message to an important figure from the past. Second, these texts contain bizarre symbolic visions that are interpreted for the prophet by the angelic mediator. Third, apocalypses contain violent repetitions. These repetitions, in other words, violate the literal sense of the text: the story cannot be mapped out chronologically. Fourth, these texts all conclude with a triumphalist note, which encourages their audiences to remain faithful despite their suffering.

Daniel as an Apocalypse

The second part of the book of Daniel (likely) marks the earliest known apocalypse. Using bizarre symbolism made up of hybrid beasts and heavenly figures, Daniel "predicts" (ex eventu) the rise and fall of empires and the events leading up to the Maccabean Revolt, showing that Antiochus would be destroyed and Israel would inherit the earth. The last details never happened, which is why most scholars have concluded the book must have been written just before Antiochus's defeat, with the author providing hope to those around him.

CHAPTER 8

Paul and the Gentile Mission

Apart from Jesus, the apostle Paul was the most important figure of early Christianity. Nearly half (thirteen) of the twenty-seven books of the New Testament claim to be written by Paul; another (Hebrews) was accepted because church fathers connected it to Paul, and Acts is primarily written about Paul. Paul was highly influential in the spread of Christianity to gentiles and the development of early Christian theology. Paul had a critical mission towards the Gentiles; however, Paul himself was considered a Pharisee.

Problems in the Study of Paul

Although we have material from Paul's hand, there are still severe difficulties in reconstructing Paul's life and teachings. The letters are vague or non-specific about a full picture of Paul. Some of the problems and concerns are because of Pseudepigrapha. Pseudepigrapha is also known as writings under a false name. It was not uncommon in the ancient world for writings to be attributed to another author or person who had a prominent name. The practice of writing under the master a person served under was not uncommon in the ancient world. Most scholars believe that elements of the New Testament letters with Paul's attribute are, in essence, pseudepigraphic.

The authorship of the Pauline corpus is divided into three groups: the Pastoral epistles (1–2 Timothy and Titus), the Deutero-Pauline epistles (Ephesians, Colossians, and 2 Thessalonians; this group is often called the "Disputed Pauline" corpus), and the undisputed Pauline letters (Romans, 1 and 2 Corinthians, Galatians, Philippians, 1 Thessalonians, and Philemon). This division occurs because of a difference in writing styles, language, and grammar.

For a more genuine understanding of Paul, it is best to stick to the latter group —(Romans, 1 and 2 Corinthians, Galatians, Philippians, 1 Thessalonians, and Philemon)—letters Paul indeed wrote.

Even these letters are highly "occasional" records of correspondence with specific communities he founded (except for Rome), addressing specific issues with specific churches. The letters are written for particular purposes. Due to the disputed nature of Paul's letters, we should not read them as systematic theological treatises but should always be aware of their context. Paul's letters are to a specific community with specific problems and not universally applied. For example, when Paul discusses circumcision, he is discussing in a specific context to specific people and not universally. Finally, Acts' account of Paul's missionary journeys and teachings seems to differ from Paul's accounts. It may be best, then, to keep in mind that Acts can tell us how Luke understood Paul, but not what Paul himself did and said due to the historical authorship and details that are varied.

A Brief Biography of Paul

Paul was born to Jewish parents, was highly educated, and lived as a devout Jew through the first part of his life. Since Paul spoke and wrote in Greek, he knew and used the Septuagint. As a Pharisee, Paul carefully followed the Jewish Law and was apocalyptically minded. During this time of his life, Paul opposed Christianity. Deeper study does not determine if Paul was against messianic Jewish believers or only Christians. Paul does not detail his conversion experience but does suggest that it involved an encounter with Jesus in his post-resurrection, bodily form. His belief in Jesus' resurrection confirmed Paul's apocalyptic views. He came to view Jesus as the first fruits of the resurrection, the sign that God had already defeated death and, therefore, the final cosmic battle between good and evil had begun.

Although many scholars wonder if Paul ever reached a consistent conclusion about the Law, it seems he did not believe that a person could become righteous by following the Law; one could become righteous only by faith in Christ. The Law was given by God and was good, but it was given as a guide for the right behavior, not a means of becoming righteous. Paul, therefore, concluded that Gentiles did not need to convert to Judaism to obtain salvation; rather, God's initial covenant with Abraham in the Jewish scriptures now included people from all nations.

After his conversion, Paul traveled widely, spreading his teachings. Paul wrote to communities he had founded but had subsequently left to continue his mission elsewhere. This correspondence represents only one side of a conversation since Paul often responded to letters he received from his churches. In many of these letters, Paul urged Christians to return to their original faith (especially when other missionaries had come preaching a different gospel) and clarified aspects of his teaching that church members had misunderstood or forgotten.

The Genre of Acts and Its Significance

The book of Acts is the first history of the church. It traces Christianity from Jesus' resurrection to the arrival of the apostle Paul in Rome. History, like any other literary genre, is told from a particular perspective. Accordingly, we can assume that Acts reflects the concerns of its author. As modern readers, then, we should approach the book of Acts as another window into Luke's view of salvation history.

The Thematic Approach to Acts

This chapter introduces another method for the study of the New Testament, the thematic approach. When scholars approach texts thematically, they look for recurring ideas that can shed light on an author's emphases. With Acts, we are particularly well-positioned to use the thematic approach because we can trace the development of particular ideas from Luke's Gospel throughout the history of the church.

From Gospel to Acts: The Opening Transition

The book of Acts narrates the missionary enterprise that began at Pentecost when the Holy Spirit came upon the Apostles and empowered them to work miracles and speak foreign languages. Just as Jesus was rejected in the Gospel, the apostles are rejected in Acts. Some Jews, however, did convert—the most important of whom was Saul, also known as Paul. It is through Paul that the Gospel was spread among Gentiles in many of the provinces of the Roman world.

Themes in the Speeches in Acts

A study of the speeches delivered to believers in Acts reveals several Lukan themes. First, Christianity is portrayed as a continuation of Judaism and, as such, the fulfillment of Scripture. Second, the Christian mission is seen as an extension of Jesus' own ministry. The center of the faith continues to be Jerusalem, the city in which the disciples were instructed to stay for a short time after Jesus' ascension.

In Acts, Luke also continues his emphasis on the sacrifice Jesus made on behalf of the world. This innocent man was a victim of injustice. God reversed this injustice, though, by raising Jesus from the dead. As we saw in the Gospel, Luke does not believe that Jesus' death itself brings atonement. Rather, the miscarriage of justice exposes guilt, which in turn brings about repentance—the necessary action for salvation.

Conclusion: The Author and His Themes in Context

These two volumes were written anonymously, though the issue of authorship is more complicated here than it is with Matthew and Mark for a number of reasons. First, these books are not completely written in the third person. In Acts, the author occasionally writes in the first person, a fact that may suggest that he was an eyewitness to some of the action. When Acts is compared to Paul's own accounts of his ministry, however, there are substantial differences. These differences call into question the attribution of these books to a companion of Paul. The first-person passages, furthermore, start and stop abruptly. It may be that the "we" passages are evidence of one of Luke's sources: a travel diary written by someone who was a companion of Paul. If this is the case, the author of Acts interjected portions of this diary into his overall narrative.

CHAPTER 9

Eighth Century Prophets: Isaiah, Amos, Hosea, Micah

The Rise of the Prophets

The rise of prophets in the biblical time was at a time to bring messages relevant from God to the people. Prophets are "spokespersons" who speak messages from God at a specific period and need. Prophets become especially prominent in the story of Israel around the time of the monarchy, primarily because they served as divine critics of political affairs. The prophets see political activities as inseparable from religious and cultic commitments and proclaim messages of divine justice against those who do what is wrong, both ethically and religiously. It is especially important to note that while Israelite prophets do make futuristic predictions, their primary function was to speak God's perspective on the present circumstances. Even their predictions are closely tied to their contexts, which makes understanding those contexts critically important for understanding their messages.

Several prophets appear in the stories of the Deuteronomistic History, empowered to deliver messages from God, with proof of their power shown by miracles they perform. Elijah and his successor Elisha (1 Kgs 17–2 Kgs 13) are the best known of these "narrative prophets." Elijah confronted the northern king Ahab over his sponsorship and worship of the Canaanite deity Baal, calling down a drought on the land that culminates in a theatrical prophetic duel on Mount Carmel between Elijah and the prophets of Baal (1 Kings 17–18). Elijah calls down fire from heaven and has the losing prophets of Baal slaughtered. Numerous stories after this event recount Elijah and Elisha were doing terrific miracles, including multiplication of food, healing of the sick, and even raising the dead. All these deeds are in the context of political critique centering on the sole worship of YHWH and the blessings and curses associated with faithfulness or unfaithfulness towards the God of Israel.

The classical prophets are those whose writings (or writings were written down by their followers and attributed to them) became part of scripture. These prophets first appear in the mid-eighth century B.C.E. (Amos, Isaiah), while the final writing prophets lived in the mid-fifth century (e.g., Malachi). Thus, these writing prophets come on the scene predicting destruction right before the Assyrians destroy Israel; others predict the destruction of Judah by the Babylonians, and others write in the wake of these tragedies, providing direction for the people. Again, a key point of emphasis is that these prophets were thoroughly focused upon their day and circumstances and were not making predictions about the twenty-first century. This chapter focuses on the prophets from before the exile(s).

Amos of Tekoa

Amos is probably the earliest of the prophetic books, with Amos's prophetic activity dating to the middle of the eighth century. Amos was from Judah but prophesied in the northern kingdom of Israel—interference unappreciated by those in power. Amos begins with stylized oracles against the various nations surrounding Israel and Judah; a move is sure to have the approval of his listeners—until he turns the accusing finger upon them, declaring that Israel is even worse off than the others because of their rebellion against God. Amos declares that God will punish Israel for its ethical violations involving issues of social injustice, raising a military attack to destroy Israel. Amos stresses that God cares more about social justice and ethical behavior—such as caring for the poor and hungry—than sacrifices or cultic worship, assuring Israel that no amount of sacrifice or religious service can compensate for injustice in the eyes of God.

Many scholars believe that a later southern redactor added the positive ending (and other positive references to Judah in the book), so the book ends not on a negative note but on the positive promise that the Davidic kingdom will be restored in utopian terms. Several features of Amos are typical of all the prophets who follow him, most notably in his demands for justice, contextually oriented predictions, the claim that the fate of the nation rests in YHWH's hands, and his notion that the God of Israel is, in fact, the God over everything and everyone, dealing justly with all.

Isaiah of Jerusalem

Isaiah of Jerusalem's career overlaps with that of Amos, covering most of the second half of the eighth century. These were years of turmoil in Judah, featuring an antagonistic relationship with Israel and the rising power of Assyria, including a lengthy siege of Jerusalem under Sennacherib in 701 B.C.E. Like Amos, Isaiah's prophecies focus on the chaotic situation in which he lived.

Most scholars have concluded that the book of Isaiah is a composite work. Although nearly all of the first thirty-nine chapters dates to the ministry of Isaiah of Jerusalem, chapter 40 marks a transition to material that seems better situated over a century and a half later, during and after the Babylonian exile. Many modern scholars thus identify three separate "Isaiahs" combined into a single work by a later redactor, giving the impression that all are from Isaiah of Jerusalem. First Isaiah (Isaiah of Jerusalem) addresses the Assyrian crisis and predicts coming judgment on the nation of Judah in chapters 1–39. Second

Isaiah (chs. 40–55) preaches consolation in the wake of judgment in the mid-sixth century. Chapters 56–66 are often identified as from Third Isaiah, a still later prophet writing after the return from Babylon. (The latter two Isaiahs are addressed in the next chapter.)

Like Amos, Isaiah preaches a message of judgment upon Israel and Judah for social and political injustice. Isaiah also contains a strong sense of hope after judgment, looking forward to a utopic restoration of Israel and Judah sometime in the future. Also like Amos, Isaiah includes oracles against other nations and empires, emphasizing that the God of Israel is, in fact, the God over the entire earth, which God judges justly.

Hosea

Hosea prophesied in the north around the same time as Amos and proclaimed God's judgment against Israel for worshiping other gods. The book focuses on Hosea's prophetic act of marrying a promiscuous woman (Gomer), whose adulterous affairs he then compares with Israel's worship of other gods. Gomer bears three children (whether these children are actually his is unclear), and he gives symbolic names to each of the children to represent the rejection of Israel's children by God (the third child is named "Lo-ammi," meaning "not my people," or more colloquially, "not mine"). Hosea takes up the form of a legal indictment, declaring that Israel would receive the penalties for breaking covenant. Israel has broken the covenant and is no longer God's special people, and God's judgment is coming swiftly. As with the other prophets, Hosea does include a few glimmers of hope, including proclamations that Israel—now no longer God's people—will one day be restored, chosen again to be God's people.

Micah

Micah is the fourth eighth-century prophet, contemporary with Hosea, Amos, and Isaiah and prophesying in the southern kingdom of Judah. Micah prophesies against both Samaria and Jerusalem, proclaiming judgment for idolatry and injustice. A few sections of the book show awareness of the Babylonian captivity and are thus likely from much later, but the majority of the book seems to have come from Micah himself. Micah 6:1–8 is especially notable as an example of a "covenantal lawsuit" in which YHWH issues a legal indictment against his people for breach of covenantal obligations. This passage is especially notable for its rejection of the idea that religious rituals could ward off God's anger, with Micah concluding with one of the great verses of the classical poets: "He has told you, O mortal, what is good: and what does the LORD require of you, but to do justice, and to love kindness, and to walk humbly with your God" (6:8).

Nahum

Unlike the other prophets so far, the three-chapter book of Nahum does not address Israel and Judah but is instead an expression of glee over the fall of the Assyrian capital Nineveh, which likely places the book around the fall of Nineveh in 612 B.C.E. Nahum declares that Nineveh is being repaid for the evil it had done and reflected the belief that YHWH is not only the God of Israel but reigns over everything.

Zephaniah

Zephaniah prophesied during the reign of Josiah (640–609 B.C.E.) and largely encapsulated many of the themes covered so far. Judah has sinned and will be punished, and the God of Israel is, in fact, the judge of the whole earth, not just Israel and Judah. Zephaniah proclaims the coming "day of YHWH," which will be a time of devastation and judgment upon Jerusalem but also upon all nations. Nevertheless, Zephaniah concludes on a strong note of hope, promising restoration after punishment.

Jeremiah

Jeremiah prophesied in the last few decades before (and sometimes beyond) the Babylonian destruction of Jerusalem in 586 B.C.E. Jeremiah declared that God was judging Judah for their unfaithfulness and that the only viable choice was to surrender to the Babylonians, who would otherwise entirely destroy Jerusalem and kill its inhabitants. This was an unpopular message, and Jeremiah was persecuted as a seditious traitor.

The Hebrew (Masoretic) version of Jeremiah upon which the traditional English versions are written is about 16 percent longer than the Septuagint version, including a quite few doublets, and is the longest book in the Bible in terms of the number of words. The book is divided into discrete sections:

Jeremiah proclaims that Judah has been even more unfaithful than Israel, reflected by social injustice and idolatry and that God is sending the Babylonians to execute judgment. He declares that there is no hope except to surrender to the Babylonians—resistance will only result in destruction and death. Even the Jerusalem Temple will offer no protection against God's judgment and will be destroyed if Judah does not submit to the Babylonians. But the news is not all bad: Jeremiah proclaims that God will ultimately restore his people, even making a "new covenant" with them that will so ingrain God's laws in their hearts that they will naturally follow God's requirements. Some scholars question whether these messages of hope are original to Jeremiah or were added by a later redactor, much like with the hopeful passages added to Amos.

Jeremiah also uses various symbolic gestures as object lessons to highlight his message, such as publicly smashing a jar or wearing a yoke on his neck. The book of Jeremiah focuses more on the person of Jeremiah than other prophetic books, highlighting his personal anguish in proclaiming such a dark and depressing message. Jeremiah complains not against his human persecutors but against God, at one point wishing that he had never been born.

Habakkuk

Habakkuk is set up as a dialogue between God and the prophet. The prophet complains about the injustice of Jerusalem, and when God replies that the Babylonians are coming to bring justice, the prophet responds that the solution is worse than the problem, that justice is not served by punishing the wicked by those even more wicked. God's response is that the Babylonians themselves will ultimately face judgment for their own evil, which appears to satisfy the prophet, as the book concludes in praise of God.

CHAPTER 10

A Creative God

Genesis is the first book of the Torah and contains some of the best-known and most influential stories of the Bible. Some even read Genesis as a scientific textbook about the world's origins and the ancestors of the faith. Although the word "Torah" is often translated "Law," it is better rendered as "instruction." Genesis provides this instruction through narratives and the lessons its stories convey. The book's English title is highly appropriate, as the book is about origins: of the world, humanity, civilization, and the nation of Israel.

Chapters 3 and 4 of the book are organized into one unit discussing Genesis 1–11 and the formation of the Pentateuch as a whole. Genesis may be divided into two parts, with the opening chapters (1–11) centering on the "cosmic origins" of the world and the second half (12–50) focusing on the beginnings of Israel. Genesis 1–11 contains a number of familiar narratives, including the creation, the Garden of Eden, and the Flood. Chapters 3 and 4 demonstrate how these opening chapters of Genesis developed and were influenced by the Middle Eastern environment in which their authors lived.

Two Creation Stories

Genesis 1–3: Some General Observations

The primary aim of Genesis chapter 3 is to examine the creation accounts from Genesis 1–3. Genesis provides two distinct creation myths, with a different vocabulary and order of events, as well as contrasting depictions of the deity. The first creation narrative (1.1–2.4a) features a six-day cycle with humans being God's last creation. These six days of work are intended to highlight the seventh day, when God rested upon the completion of his work. Thus, the first creation account establishes divine cosmic origins for the sabbath day. It is also important to note that in this account, God does not create the universe out of nothing. Instead, this version clearly indicates that the cosmos was formed out of untamed, though preexisting, matter.

The second creation account (2.4b–3.24) is very different from the first. There is no description of the creation of the earth or the heavens. The only action described in detail is the creation of the first man and the first woman. Moreover, humans do not come into being by God's words alone in this account; rather, God is a craftsman who forms the first man out of clay and the first woman from his rib. Finally, the second creation myth details the lives of the first humans by including the Garden of Eden narrative.

God's motives for the creation of humans are also different in each account. In the first myth, humans are created to have dominion over the earth and all of its creatures. In the second, God's creation of humans is connected to agriculture and the need for someone to "till and keep the garden." Finally, each narrative presents a very different picture of the creator. In Genesis 1.1–2.4a God is a distant or remote figure who can produce just by speaking. The God of Genesis 2.4b–3.24 is more accessible and anthropomorphic. Also, God is called by different names in the two stories, referred to as "God" in the first narrative and as "the lord God" in the second. Taken in sum, all of these differences suggest that these accounts were written by two authors and that the second narrative was included as a way of answering some basic questions about human experience and existence.

The Primeval History

Genesis can be divided into two parts. The first eleven chapters contain the Primeval History, which tells of the events at the beginning of time. Genesis 1 gives the famous account of God's creation of the world through a series of ten events over seven days. Genesis 2–3 features the story of Adam and Eve and the forbidden fruit. Other vital stories include Cain's murder of his brother

Abel (ch. 4), Noah's Flood (chs. 6–9), and the Tower of Babel (ch. 11).

The Primeval History as Meaningful Stories

The Genesis creation stories were not written from a modern scientific perspective, and the rest of the Primeval History presents similar challenges, such as extraordinarily long lives, seeming contradictions (e.g., Cain building a city), and unverifiable supernatural events. Rather than reading them as scientific and historical accounts, these stories should be read as myths, stories that try to make sense of the world and our place in it. As such, these stories convey very powerful lessons, regardless of their correspondence with history. These stories emphasize things like the supremacy of humanity, the importance of the Sabbath day, and the importance of obedience to God.

The Ancestral History

The remaining chapters (12–50) comprise the Ancestral History, which tells the stories of Israel's ancestors, focusing especially on the figures of Abraham, Isaac, Jacob, and Joseph. Many modern scholars have questioned the historicity of these stories on the basis of anachronisms, internal inconsistencies, and doublets.

These narratives explain the origins of Israel and set up the events of Exodus while also staking Israel's claim to the land as divinely promised and provided. On a more individual level, these stories also provide ethical guidance for how individual Israelites are to live, guidance especially illustrated in the Joseph novella, where both Joseph's integrity in a foreign land and God's oversight of his life, bringing good out of tragedy, receive special emphasis.

Influences from the Near East

Although the creation accounts in Genesis highlight beliefs and practices (for example, monotheism and the sabbath) that were particular to ancient Israel, it is important to remember that no text is created in a vacuum; the books of the Bible are no exception. There are several other creation myths from the Near East that bear striking similarities to the Genesis narratives, including the Babylonian myth *Enuma Elish*, which shares a number of affinities with Genesis 1. These include the creative powers of the deity, the formation of the cosmos out of existing matter (Tiamat's body), and the creation of humans in the "likenesses" of the god(s).

While Genesis 2.4b–3.24 has a different style and theme from 1.1–2.4a, it too has Near Eastern antecedents. These include the formation of man out of soil and the creation of humans for the purpose of working the earth. More important, there are possible parallels between the Eden account in Genesis and *Gilgamesh*, such as the attainment of knowledge and the inevitable fear of mortality.

Moreover, although the biblical texts do appear to borrow themes from Near Eastern literature, the Genesis accounts are also innovative since they adapt, transform, and reject many aspects of Near Eastern mythology. A good example of this is the demythologizing of the battle before creation in Genesis 1.

Above all, this chapter on Genesis 1–3 and its parallel literature illustrates that there is a great deal of room for interpretation and critique within both the creation stories and the Bible as a whole. These three chapters of Genesis demonstrate that there were different views or schools of thought present in ancient Israel; in future chapters we will encounter even more examples of this diversity.

The Challenges Posed by Science and History to the Understanding of Genesis

Genesis is an ancient book that reflects an ancient worldview; many of the accounts of the Primeval History do not line up with modern scientific knowledge. For example, the first creation story talks about evening and morning happening before the creation of sun, moon, or stars—and vegetation is created on earth before there was a sun. The geological record (and the quantity of available water) also contradicts the account of a flood that covered the entire earth. The Primeval History also includes numerous problems, such as the implausibly long lives of the early humans and internal inconsistencies in many of the stories. The Ancestral History also includes anachronisms, internal inconsistencies, and doublets—all of which are typical in collections of oral tradition. The stories of Genesis reflect the ancient context in which they were produced. The stories of Genesis are best understood not as historical narratives but as a collection of ancient myths and legends put together to help the Israelites to understand their place in the world.

Genesis Authorship Discussions

The first part of this chapter discusses how repetitions or variant discussions of the same subject matter (doublets) within the biblical text indicate that more than one writer is responsible for the authorship of the Pentateuch. The second part of the chapter focuses on Genesis 4–11 and its accounts of early human, post-creation history before Abraham. The primary goal is to expand the discussion of the Documentary Hypothesis and to apply it to Genesis 4–11. This chapter also shows how the Flood narratives, like the creation myths in Genesis 1–3, borrow heavily from the antecedent Flood narratives of Israel's Near Eastern neighbors.

History of Scholarship

The traditional view on the authorship of the Pentateuch is that Moses himself composed all five books. By the seventeenth century this view was challenged primarily on the basis that there were too many inconsistencies and repetitions within the text. The great methodological innovations for biblical interpretation came about in the eighteenth and nineteenth centuries. Although Jean Astruc agreed that Moses authored the Pentateuch, he also posited that the overall disparities between the creation narratives (including the different names of God in each) suggested that Moses was using two distinct sources when he wrote Genesis 1–3.

The most significant contribution came from Julius Wellhausen, who, drawing on the work of many others, developed the Documentary Hypothesis as a means of sorting out the variations and repetitions present in the Pentateuch. In sum, the Documentary Hypothesis states that the Pentateuch was formed by four distinct sources known as J, E, D, and P. While many aspects of Wellhausen's work are highly problematic, the basic conclusion that there were four separate voices that contributed to the formation of the Torah became a mainstay in biblical scholarship.

This chapter also points out some of the major critiques and adaptations of the Documentary Hypothesis. Scholars have found fault with the dating of the Pentateuchal sources and the number of distinct, identifiable sources. Although the evidence does not fit as neatly into the classical formulation of the hypothesis as scholars at one time thought, almost all biblical scholars recognize that the repetitions, inconsistencies, and contradictions in the Pentateuch are best explained by the existence of distinct sources dating to different historical periods.

The second part of this chapter further illustrates these issues of authorship as it covers the narrative of chapters 4–11 of Genesis. Using the Documentary Hypothesis as a starting point, it is possible to see two separate sources for Genesis 4–11. The J and P sources are often presented separately in distinct and uninterrupted blocks of text. For example, Genesis 11.1–9 is made up entirely of the J source, while 11.10–26 is exclusively P. In other places, such as the Flood narrative, J and P are blended together, demonstrating the complexities of a redactor's work.

Primeval History

Genesis 4–11 continues the biblical account of early human history after the creation narrative. Throughout these chapters, the J source presents recurring themes describing the ever-deteriorating human condition and the widening gap between the evils of the world and the golden age of Eden. These themes include a worsening relationship between humans and the soil, an increased alienation between God and humans, and the increasing evil of humanity as a whole.

Genesis 4–11 also contains genealogies from both the J and P sources. However, J and P utilize genealogies in different ways. The J genealogies (Genesis 4 and 10) are segmented and act as a vehicle for launching into narratives about several different personalities, including Cain and Abel's descendants. The P genealogies are concerned with continuity, demonstrating the familial connections from Adam to Abraham. Furthermore, the P genealogies and the J material in Genesis 4–11 as a whole both seem to point to a similar conclusion: humans and life on earth in general were getting increasingly worse. P does this by showing that the life spans of the biblical figures were getting successively shorter, and presumably more corrupt, with each passing generation.

The Flood

The account of Noah and the Flood is one of the most familiar stories from the Bible. Beyond the rather stern moral message about God's punishment of wickedness, this passage is also a model of how the Documentary Hypothesis works. Up to this point in Genesis, the J and P sources have appeared separately, one after another. In Genesis 6.5–9.17 the two sources are interconnected and woven together. Despite these complications, J can usually be identified by its style and language, including the use of the name "Yahweh" for God and the continued use of vivid anthropomorphisms, as we saw in J's creation story. P too is recognizable by its use of *elohim* instead of Yahweh as well as its descriptions of the Flood as an undoing of creation and a renewal of creation after the deluge.

Near Eastern Parallels

In addition to the complexities of the sources in Genesis 6.5–9.17, the Flood story, much like the creation accounts, shares many affinities with its Near Eastern counterparts. Stories of a great Flood were prevalent in many ancient societies, and some have questioned whether other cultures borrowed from the biblical narrative. However, dating indicates that the Babylonian epics, including *Atra-hasis* and the pertinent sections of *Gilgamesh*, were earlier and undoubtedly influenced the biblical writers.

Implications for Our Study

Despite its limitations, the Documentary Hypothesis has helped open up critical discussion on the Pentateuch for both scholars and students alike. Critical methods of interpretation enable us to appreciate the inclusion of repetitions and alternative accounts within the biblical texts as a demonstration of the pluralism in ancient Israel. The ability to identify common themes and vocabulary within these sources also gives us a better understanding of their development and possible history. The first eleven chapters of Genesis retell myths of origins known from other ancient Near Eastern peoples and introduce themes that will be developed further as the narrative continues.

Sabbath

"Remember the sabbath day, and keep it holy. Six days you shall labor [melakhah] and do all your work. But the seventh day is a sabbath to the Lord your God; you shall not do any work—you, your son or your daughter, your male or female slave, your livestock, or the alien resident in your towns. For in six days the Lord made heaven and earth, the sea, and all that is in them, but rested [menuchah] the seventh day; therefore the Lord blessed the sabbath day and consecrated it." Exodus 20:8-11 (NRSV)

Biblically, we forget that the foundation of working and resting in Exodus 20:8-11 centers around two Hebrew words: melakhah (work) vs. menuchah (rest).

These two root Hebrew words melakhah and menuchah found in Exodus 20:8-11 define productive labor and rest (abstention from melakhah) within the Decalogue; however, many misunderstandings of these words is applied creating modern cultural anomalies dictating what we can and cannot do on Sabbath. The Bible validates melakhah, telling us that we should engage melakhah six days of the week (Ex. 20:9; Deut. 5:13), but that the seventh day is different because it is blessed (mevorakah) and holy (kadosh).

The Hebrew word melakhah means more than just labor. In fact, in order to make the Sabbath holy, one must refrain from any activity which is creative (because God rested from His creative activities), or otherwise makes changes to our environment.

While this may seem like basic Seventh-day Adventist theology, the application of melakhah has been seen beyond God's creative acts with the focus on an ill-conceived definition of resting.

For six days, God created everything from nothing. When applying a definition of productive labor (melakhah) and abstention from productive labor in life (menuchah), a case can be made that we are to build the Kingdom of Christ for six days by prescription as believers. Building the Kingdom of Christ for six days a week is a creative act that is, indeed, requiring all our effort to make new disciples. As Adventists, we could, in theory, be having one day in which we cease from creating in our most earnest actions the Kingdom of God with our human might. This can be said for all people who work as they are to be building Christ's Kingdom in all their creative actions.

In Mark 3:1-6, Jesus was questioned regarding the legitimacy of healing on Sabbath, which became part of rabbinical law later in Mishna Yoma 8.6. Jesus' actions negated creating anew on the Sabbath by restoring a person (Mark 3:5) to their original created design, which did not violate biblical law. Jesus did not create on the Sabbath, but rather, he restored.

The development of Jewish law in Mishna Shabbat 7:2 demonstrated that oral and rabbinical writings added 39 categories for Shabbat restrictions during the time of the Second Temple, based on the activities that were involved in the building of the Tabernacle. The original intent of the restrictions revolving creative work centered on the work delegated in the Tabernacle, which most people incorrectly transpose into other areas of spirituality. The negative mitzvoth (commandments) for Sabbath punishment are in regard to creating holiness in the Tabernacle and the roles people had.

In order to understand how to rest in Exodus 20:8-11 is defined in the biblical mind, menuchah must be defined in terms of cessation from work. The word menuchah is from nuah (to rest, to repose, to be quiet). It is the same root that produces Noah, the name of the man who brought rest to the world (although, obviously, not the way the world expected). Why do we care about this little correction? Because the rabbis connected this word, menuchah, with the Sabbath. To the biblical mind, menuchah is the same as happiness and stillness, as peace and harmony. It is the state in which there is no strife and no fighting, no fear, and no distrust. The essence of the good life is summed up in menuchah. In later times, menuchah became a synonym for the life in the world to come, for eternal life. This is the eschaton in modern thought found in Revelation 16:11, in the third angel's message. Adventist theology keenly points out the importance of a global-wide menuchah in prophetic reference.

All of the restrictions placed around Sabbath, in order to protect the sanctity and holiness of Sabbath, are further developed by the prophets who sought to protect the two greatest concepts in the Fourth Commandment: to not create anew and to be in a state of non-creation.

As an example, using exaggerated polarization, I will provide examples of common characteristics providing a difference between both melakhah and menuchah.

Melakhah is about changing things; Menuchah is about stability.

Melakhah is about tension; Menuchah is about relaxation.

Melakhah is about needs and desires; Menuchah is about getting in touch with what we have.

Melakhah is respected and prized within biblical interpretation centering around the Fourth Commandment. The world is to be built, and that's what melakhah is all about.

The problem arises when people are unable to leave the world of melakhah and, in fact, become its slave; people become slaves to creative work.

In the New Testament, the story of Jesus and the Pharisees, regarding the plucking of heads of grain on the Sabbath, must be read through a historical lens focusing on the Second Temple period. This story most likely takes place after the festival of Passover, due to the harvest. Non-Sabbath keeping Protestant Christianity incorrectly states that Jesus uses Mark 2:24-28 to revoke the rules of Sabbath and the keeping of the Commandments. Jesus is not eating grain to save a life; it was insinuated that David did, in the Temple. The verse reads:

The Pharisees said to him, "Look, why are they doing what is unlawful on the Sabbath?" He answered, "Have you never read what David did when he and his companions were hungry and in need?

In the days of Abiathar the high priest, he entered the house of God and ate the consecrated bread, which is lawful only for priests to eat. And he also gave some to his companions. Then he said to them, "The Sabbath was made for man, not man for the Sabbath; so the Son of man is lord even of the Sabbath." Mark 2:24-28

Reading the story in light of biblical understanding during the Second Temple, Jesus is juxtaposing the intellectual thought found in the Fourth Commandment with the standards of lawful Sabbath adherence of his time.

Jewish law allowed Temple service to supersede Sabbath prohibitions. Jesus' profound statement during his lifetime acknowledges that Sabbath is used to heal, restore, and abstain from the world being dominated by humanity. Sabbath cannot condemn humanity. Sabbath can only provide peace from the creative work.

If we can turn our theology to a historical application, I think we would see our modern hermeneutical problems concerning activities that we approve Friday night or Saturday are created by our own misunderstandings. Instead of focusing on creating a kingdom of believers for six days, we instead put all our church activities on Saturday in order to make Sabbath different than the other six. The outcome is a form of Sabbath culture that seeks to set standards for Sabbath, for example: no wading in water past your knees—or else it is considered swimming; instead of playing competitive sports, engage only in peaceful, non-competitive activities, preferably in nature; no secular music, film or television; and make sure we fill the Sabbath hours with church activities.

This methodology is destructive because it focuses on presumptions and technical interpretations, which may eclipse the true meaning of the Sabbath while attempting to replace Biblical Sabbath blessings and prohibitions with traditions of humankind.

An Orthodox Jewish rabbi recently challenged, "If you want to worship the Sabbath, become an Adventist.

If you want to worship God who made Sabbath, talk to me instead…" His point is precisely that—we, as Adventists, too often worship the Sabbath above the one who created it.

Who Killed Jesus

The Pittsburgh Synagogue shooting occurred at the Tree of Life, also known as the L'Simcha Congregation, in the Squirrel Hill neighborhood of Pittsburgh, Pennsylvania, on October 27, 2018, during Sabbath morning services. The terrorist killed eleven people, and seven were injured. In February 2019, a centuries-old Jewish cemetery in the small village of Quatzenheim, in northeastern France, was vandalized in the night. Some 96 tombs were spray-painted with blue swastikas.

These are only a couple of examples. Around the world, there is a rise in antisemitism. The reasons, historically, are many, but here is one that can be attributed to Christians: the continuing belief that the Jews killed Jesus.

Twenty-six percent of Americans still believe that the Jews killed Jesus, according to a 2013 survey by the Anti-Defamation League. The actual figure is undoubtedly higher because people are often reluctant to admit they hold politically incorrect views or unaccepted opinions. How many people would admit to being racist, even if indeed they are?

Christians need to stop antisemitism. We can begin by not blaming the Jews for killing Jesus. It is wrong. It is a lie. Christians have a responsibility to seek truth and stop propagating untruths. Practicing religious Jews did not kill Jesus.

The Jewish Populace Liked Jesus

Many accounts in the New Testament show how much the people loved Jesus and welcomed him. Jesus makes that very point to the arresting party in the Garden of Gethsemane explaining that he would sit every day in the Temple teaching and was not seized or arrested (Matthew 26:55; Mark 14:48-49; Luke 22:52-53; cf. John 18:20). Jesus' popularity was so great, that as he taught and healed, the throngs grew and "there was a great multitude of his disciples, and a great crowd of people from all Judea and Jerusalem and the coastal region of Tyre and Sidon [Lebanon], and all the people were trying to touch him" (Luke 6:17,19).

With a great parallel to other Jewish teachers, Jesus taught in the Temple courtyards like that of Rabbi Yohanan ben Zakkai, who used to "sit and teach daily in the shade of the sanctuary" (Babylonian Talmud, Pesahim 26a). The Jews accepted Jesus, and he was popular among the people (Matthew 9:33). The Gospel of Matthew explains that the Jewish leadership feared a riot if they dared to arrest Jesus at a public gathering — that the "multitude" of Jews would rise to defend him. (Matt. 26:3-5).

So Then, Who Didn't Like Jesus?

The Sadducees and Joseph Caiaphas did not like Jesus. Joseph Caiaphas was the High Priest of Jerusalem who, according to Biblical accounts, sent Jesus to Pilate for his execution. Caiaphas was the son-in-law of Annas, the high priest from 6 to 15 CE and the head of a family that would control the high priesthood for most of the first century. Annas is mentioned in biblical accounts (Luke 3:2; Acts 4:1-22). As a high priest and chief religious authority in the land, Caiaphas had many essential responsibilities, including controlling the temple treasury, managing the temple police and other personnel, performing religious rituals, and serving as president of the Sanhedrin (rabbinical court).

The high priest had another, more controversial function in first-century Jerusalem: he served as a sort of liaison between Roman authority and the Jewish population. High priests, drawn from the Sadducean aristocracy, received their appointment from Rome since the time of Herod the Great, and Rome looked to high priests to keep the Jewish populace in line. We know from other cases (such as one incident in 66 CE) that Roman prefects demanded that high priests arrest and turn over Jews seen as agitators.

For ten years, Caiaphas served with Roman prefect Pontius Pilate. The two presumably had a close relationship. Caiaphas' motives in turning Jesus over to Pilate are a subject of speculation. Some historians suggest that he had little choice. Others argue that Caiaphas saw Jesus as a threat to the existing religious order. Many Jews resented the close relationship that the high priest maintained with Roman authorities and suspected them of taking bribes or practicing other forms of corruption.

In the year 36 CE, both Caiaphas and Pilate were dismissed from office by Syrian governor, Vitellius, according to the Jewish historian Josephus. Josephus described the high priests of the family of Annas as "heartless when they sit in judgment."

Luke 23:1 describes how the seventy-one members of the Sanhedrin, plus elders, rabbis, and other officials, took Jesus to Pilate. The physical size of the Sanhedrin is small. Modern archaeology finds the ruins of the Sanhedrin to be standing-room-only for a small group of people. Therefore, only a small number of Jewish people actually sought to remove Jesus.

Did the Jews Kill Jesus?

In poring over the gospels for an answer, I was surprised to discover that few if any Jews were present at the trial and condemnation of Jesus, other than the Jewish officials: "And they led Jesus away to the high priest: and with him assembled all the chief priests and the elders and the scribes" (Mark 14:53; Luke 22:54; Matthew 26:57). The story does provide us with details on how the minority of the Roman-appointed Sadducee leadership first encountered Jesus during Passover. John 18:13 tells us that first, they took him to Annas, who was the father-in-law of Caiaphas, the high priest that year.

Passover Rituals

Besides the fact that Jews did not crucify people, the Passover rituals don't allow ceremonially clean Jews to kill someone during the festival. The primary sources available estimate that the population living in Jerusalem during the time of Jesus was probably around 80,000 to 100,000 citizens. The number of practicing Jews from the Diaspora visiting for the mandatory feast and festival of Passover would place the number of those in Jerusalem in the hundreds of thousands. There are an estimated three million people, both Jews and Gentiles, who visited Jerusalem for the Passover during the time of Jesus. According to Josephus, Hecataeus of Abdera wrote in the fourth century BC that 120,000 men inhabited Jerusalem. Josephus also said that there were 2,700,000 people within the walls of Jerusalem when the Romans, under Titus, besieged it in 70 CE.

The Bible tells us in John 18:28 that when the elders and leaders took Jesus from Caiaphas to Pilate's headquarters that it was early in the morning. We must also remember that the Jews would not enter the headquarters of Pilate in order to avoid ritual defilement, which would prevent them from eating the Passover. The millions of practicing Jews who were in Jerusalem during the Passover would not be breaking their ritual cleanliness by associating with a non-Jew or condemning someone to death because they would have to redo their temple sacrifice. This is not feasible or possible because the Temple slaughter of an animal takes a long period of time, notwithstanding that millions are in line all day long slaughtering their Passover lambs.

Antisemitism in Story Transmission

It is unlikely that ordinary Jews were in attendance at the trial of Jesus. Jesus' arrest was a clandestine operation. Only select Jewish officials knew about it. It was Passover eve, and Jews were busy with purification and other preparations for the festival. They were not en masse yelling to kill Jesus. The practicing Jews could not, and would not, defile Passover.

So antisemitism has been propagated because of poorly translated theology.

A troublesome mistranslated verse found in Matthew 27:24-25 has erroneously blamed the Jews for over a millennium for killing Jesus. However, it never should have. Pilate pronounced that Jesus was guilty under Roman authority. Matthew 27:24-25 states, "So when Pilate saw that he could do nothing, but rather that a riot was beginning, he took some water and washed his hands before the crowd, saying, 'I am innocent of this man's blood; see to it yourselves.' Then the people as a whole answered, 'His blood be on us and on our children!'"

Even Pope Benedict XVI repudiates the accusations against the Jews. In his 2011 book Jesus of Nazareth, he acknowledges the translation of ochlos in Matthew to mean the "crowd," rather than the Jewish people. This follows modern objective translations and changes the perception of who killed Jesus. It cannot be the Jews, for those in the crowd could not be practicing Jews—or else they would not have been there, but rather in their own homes for the Passover holiday.

Judeans, Not Jews

The translation of "Jew" and "Judean" in the book of John is pivotal to understanding who killed Jesus. Ioudaios is an ancient Greek ethnonym used in classical and biblical literature which commonly translates to "Jew" or "Judean." The choice of translation is the subject of various scholarly debates, given its central importance to ancient literature. The word is used primarily in three areas of literature in antiquity: the later books of the Hebrew Bible (e.g., the Books of the Maccabees), the New Testament (particularly the Gospel of John and Acts of the Apostles), and classical writers from the region such as Josephus and Philo. Translating Ioudaios as "Jews" has implications about the people—the term the "Jews" (Ioudaios) functions as a hostile collective stereotype and is identified with evil and the devil—whereas translation as "Judeans" emphasizes a geographical origin, which could include people of other ethnicities, such as Romans.

In John 2:13, a Passover is mentioned together with the fact that Jesus and his disciples went up to Jerusalem for this occasion. Here, according to John 2:14–22, the cleansing of the temple takes place. Thus, we find Jesus active in the center of Jewish faith and religion. Jesus' move to Judea in 3:22 means Jesus took a step outside of this religious center; he and his disciples move towards the land of Ioudaia (εἰς τὴν Ἰουδαίαν γῆν). The expression is striking because it is unique in the New Testament. In John, the term Ἰουδαία seems to refer to Judea, the territory of the tribe of Judah. This becomes evident by the concept of "land," which is added in 3:22, in comparison with other parts of Israel such as Samaria and Galilee, to which Jesus moves afterward (4:3–54). In 3:22 the double term might also point to the rural area outside Jerusalem belonging to the southern part of Israel.

So the use of Ἰουδαῖος in John shows that Ioudaios in passages like John 3:25 is more accurately read as "Judean" rather than "Jew."

Conclusion

The problems of retelling the Passion week story often include wrongfully victimizing an entire group of people.

This victimization has perpetuated violence, hatred, and genocide. Let's stop saying, "The Jews killed Jesus." When scripture speaks of "Jews," we should be careful not to victimize a people, when it is actually speaking of a geographical group from Judea, composed of Jews and Gentiles.

Discussions of Women in Paul

Women in Paul's Churches

Paul's undisputed letters indicate that women played a role in the foundation of the earliest churches. In his letter to Rome, Paul mentions Phoebe (a deacon), Prisca, Mary, Tryphaena, Tryphosa, Persis, Julia, the mother of Rufus, and the sister of Nereus. He also mentions Junia and names her as "foremost among the apostles." In addition, several of Paul's other letters suggest the importance of women in the early church.

Some women in Pauline churches took to heart Paul's ascetic message and renounced marriage. Later letters written in Paul's name attempt to stem this interpretation and reassert traditional roles for women.

Women Associated with Jesus

Although Jesus' closest disciples were men, the earliest Gospel traditions make clear that there were many women associated with Jesus. In addition to traveling with Jesus, these women provided financial support for his ministry. Women accompanied Jesus from Galilee to Jerusalem and were present at his crucifixion. They were also the first witnesses to the empty tomb, and thus the first to proclaim Jesus' resurrection.

Jesus' association with women may be historically credible in part because of his apocalyptic views. Since part of his message was the reversal of fortunes, it is possible that Jesus' association with women—a part of society generally perceived to be inferior—was an enactment of his apocalyptic message.

Paul's Understanding of Women in the Church

Although Paul's message may appear radical in its egalitarianism, he does not urge a social revolution. In fact, Paul urges his followers to stay within their socially defined roles and wait for the parousia. Equality in Christ, therefore, does not necessitate equality in society.

Women in the Aftermath of Paul

Since Paul's views of women were ambivalent—women could serve in the church but must retain their social status as women—it is not surprising that several Christian groups subsequently used Paul to advance their own views. One group took the position that women were equal to men in every way. Other Christians, however, argued that women should marry and occupy a traditional submissive role.

Ancient Ideologies of Gender

In antiquity, most people thought men and women were different in degree, not in kind. There was one continuum of humanity. On the upper end of the scale were men—those individuals who, for a variety of reasons, had been formed perfectly in the womb—and on the lower end of the scale were women—those, conversely, who were imperfectly formed. Since women were viewed as under-developed men, they were quite literally the weaker sex and were expected to assume a social role in line with this weakness.

Gender Ideology and the Pauline Churches

Many Christian converts in the early centuries were women. This may not be surprising, since Christian communities did not initially gather in large public spaces but rather in private homes where women had influence and authority. As long as Christians met within the confines of the home, women were able to hold positions of authority and prominence.

As the movement grew, however, Christianity became more public, and it became problematic for women to retain their leadership positions. As a result of the tension between public and private, some Christians argued that societal constructions of sex were not valid for those who were in Christ. These Christians urged freedom from marital constraints, claiming that it was Christ who had set them free. According to this view, women should continue leading communities, since they were equal to men in Christ.

This is not, however, the view that ultimately won. Movements seeking absolute equality of women in the Christian community were opposed based on assumptions of "natural" and "unnatural" acts and spheres. When the apocalyptic fervor began to subside, Christians no longer waited anxiously for the end but began to establish a church hierarchy to guide them in appropriate Christian behavior. Public activity came to be the job of men, and women were taught to be modest, quiet, and submissive.

APPENDIX 4

The rise of AntiJudaism

When scholars refer to the "catholic" epistles (Hebrews; James; 1 and 2 Peter; 1, 2, and 3 John; and Jude), they use the term "catholic" to mean "general" or "universal." The catholic epistles were not written to specific communities with specific problems. Rather, they address universal issues in Christianity.

Early Christian Self-Definition

All social groups establish criteria by which individuals are measured as a means of defining group boundaries. Christianity eventually sought an identity independent of Jews, who did not believe Jesus was the messiah. The development of this identity is apparent in some early Christian writings.

Continuity and Superiority: The Epistle to the Hebrews

Although Hebrews is often called a letter, it does not contain an epistolary prescript, name the author or the addressees, or include an opening prayer or thanksgiving. It is more likely an early Christian homily or treatise. The book is anonymous, although it has traditionally been attributed to Paul. The emphases and language in the book, however, are not Pauline.

The epistle to the Hebrews asserts the superiority of Christ to the prophets, the angels, Moses, Joshua, and the Jewish priesthood. Christ brings a superior covenant, brings a superior tabernacle, and makes a superior sacrifice. Like many other authors whose task is Christian self-definition, this author uses the Hebrew Scriptures to illustrate the authenticity of his claims. For example, he cites the prophet Jeremiah's prediction that God will make a new covenant with Israel and Judah. Drawing on Platonic thought, this author argues that the old covenant was a foreshadowing of the new, an imperfect reflection of a perfect reality.

Scholars do not know when or where this book was written. It is clear, though, that the author is concerned about defining group boundaries. He argues that Christianity represents the perfection of Judaism. Christianity is the religion foretold by the prophets. Those who do not believe that Jesus was the messiah, moreover, are not the true people of God.

Discontinuity and Supremacy: The *Epistle of Barnabas*

Rather than seeing Judaism as the foreshadowing of Christianity, *Barnabas* portrays Judaism as a false religion.

According to this author, the Jews broke their covenant as soon as they received it. Whereas the author of Hebrews claims that the Old Testament contains prophecies of the new covenant and its perfection of Judaism, *Barnabas* claims that the Old Testament is not a Jewish book but a Christian one.

The *Epistle of Barnabas* received its name from early Christians who suggested that it was written by Paul's companion Barnabas. Modern scholars, though, believe that the book was written long after Barnabas's death, perhaps around 130 C.E. The book was included in the New Testament in parts of Egypt through the fourth century.

Barnabas accuses the Jews of misunderstanding the Old Testament: they rely on a literal reading of the text, but its meaning is apparent only through allegory. *Barnabas*, however, does not completely do away with literal interpretations: the story of Moses breaking the tablets of the Law is, according to *Barnabas*, a true account that reflects the broken covenant between the Jews and God.

Barnabas defines Christianity by rejecting the authenticity of all Jewish claims. Christianity does not stand in continuity with historic Judaism but is nonetheless the rightful heir to Israel's promises. The Old Testament, furthermore, belongs solely to Christians; the Jews have no right to claim it.

Conclusion: The Rise of Christian Anti-Judaism

The authors of Hebrews and *Barnabas*, as well as those of other early Christian anti-Jewish books, sought to justify their beliefs in the face of the much larger and more recognized religion of Judaism. While Christian tradition began by defining itself as the inheritor of God's promises, by the second century, some Christians began to claim that Judaism was a false and misguided religion. Christians rejected a connection with Judaism but continued to affirm their relationship to the promises in the Old Testament. For these Christian authors, the anti-Jewish rhetoric was an attempt to distinguish Christianity from Judaism.